WRITING

Total Solutions for Teachers

Grade 1

by
Lori De Goede

Published by
Frank Schaffer Publications®

Author: Lori De Goede
Editor: Karen Thompson
Interior Designer: Teather Uhrik

Frank Schaffer Publications®

Send all inquiries to:
Frank Schaffer Publications
3195 Wilson Drive NW
Grand Rapids, Michigan 49544

Writing: Total Solutions for Teachers—grade 1

ISBN: 0-7682-3101-9

1 2 3 4 5 6 7 8 9 10 MAZ 10 09 08 07 06 05

Table of Contents

Introduction

This book is divided into the five major areas of the writing process. They are brainstorming, drafting, revising, editing, and publishing. The book also focuses on strategies within each section that include direct instruction, modeling, practiced, and projects. Because teaching the writing process varies greatly between students in first grade and students in much higher grades, the emphasis on this book is the steps of the writing process illustrated and culminating through monthly projects. The modeling pages are teacher-directed and focus on the teacher modeling modeling the steps of the writing process to students.

Writing with first-grade students at this age, can be a challenge! Some students will find writing a complicated process. Many students continue to struggle with forming letters correctly, and most do not understand writing conventions. Despite these factors, it is very important to begin teaching your students how the writing process works. If they learn it at a younger age, they will not have to break bad habits in their future writing. This book will provide you with many activities and projects to introduce your students to the writing process.

To make this process successful, it is important for you to

- share your own excitement for writing
- share various examples of different types of writing
- provide enough time for your students to write
- write together often—are a great writing role model
- take only select pieces of writing through the complete writing process
- create a purpose for writing by having your students share their writing
- maintain an environment that is free of criticism and competition and where ideas are valued and there is freedom to take risks

What Is Brainstorming?

Brainstorming Is...

- generating a list of writing topics
- narrowing down what topic to write about
- "warming up" your brain to write about a specific topic
- deciding what details about the topic to include in the writing
- organizing your thoughts about the topic

5

Brainstorming

Brainstorming on a topic is almost second nature to adults, but first-grade students need to be shown how to think about a topic and organize their thoughts. You may want to make an overhead transparency of some of the practice pages and complete the activity together before having your students practice the skill. Below are a few suggestions to model brainstorming.

Daily News

It is helpful to do this writing activity on an easel with the students sitting on the floor. First, share what you will be doing for the day and make some notes. Have the students generate sentences about the day from the notes you have taken. You will be doing the writing, so you can model appropriate spacing, penmanship, and punctuation. Have the students help you sound out the spelling of the words—this allows you to focus on specific phonics rules with them.

A Picture Is Worth a Thousand Words

Have your students draw a picture of their topic before starting to write. This will help them to begin to organize their thoughts. It gives them something visual to look at while they are trying to elaborate on their writing topic.

Character/Setting Cards

A fun way to jump-start the brainstorming process is to have the students randomly choose a character and setting for their story from a set of character/setting cards. To make these cards, write different characters and settings on index cards—it is helpful to use two different colors to keep them separated. Place the character cards in one basket and the setting cards in another, and then allow each student to pick one of each. It is also helpful to have the students work in pairs to share their plans for their stories.

Brainstorming (cont.)

Shared Experience Writing

It is important to write about things you know and care about. Field trips and special events are great group writing topics because each person has shared in the experience. As a group, write notes about the experience. Then each student can use the notes to aid in his or her writing.

Current Events

Along with shared experiences, great writing topics always spring up in the world and in your community. After discussing the known information about a specific current event and taking some notes, the students can write their perspective or share what they know about the event (like a newspaper or television reporter).

Book-related Writing

Sharing a great picture book with your students is another wonderful way to spark a writing topic. After reading the book, jot down a few notes about the story to get the students ready to write about the topic. In many stories, the character encounters a problem that needs to be solved. These specific problems can cause your students to come up with alternative solutions for what they would do in the character's situation. See the list of book-related writing topics on pages 138–140.

Brainstorming (cont.)

Share the Pen

While you are showing your students how to organize their thoughts on a topic, you want to get them involved. You will do the majority of the writing (for time's sake), but it is helpful to have the students participate in the process. Most of your students will be eager to share the pen, so they will be actively involved in the lesson.

"Talk-Through" Brainstorming

It is very important for teachers to verbalize their thought processes so the students get an idea of how "talk-through" brainstorming works. During this process, you need to talk to yourself, not the students. They need to see how you are working things out in your head as they hear what you are thinking.

Use a Variety of Graphic Organizers

Graphic organizers are great ways to gather and record information on a topic. There are many examples of graphic organizers in this book. You will want to use these organizers as a class to help your first-grade students become familiar with these helpful writing tools.

Seasonal/Topic Word Banks

Many young students dislike writing because they only have a small bank of known words that they are able write. Often, first-grade students get hung up on sounding out hard, unknown words they encounter as they are reading, and in turn, writing. Until they have more experience with words and begin to add to their writing vocabulary, it is helpful to have word banks for the students to use when writing about specific topics. A great way to incorporate these into your classroom is to generate words on a current writing topic with your students and write them on a related poster (this can be a blank poster with pictures of the topic or a poster that is a specific shape). Display these around your classroom so your students are surrounded by words they can use when they write.

Sky Words
blue
clouds
birds flying

Brainstorming (cont.)

Class Word Books

These are similar to the seasonal/topic word banks but do not require a lot of wall space. If you find that you need to consolidate a large quantity of word banks, you could type the lists and put them into books for the students to flip through when looking for words. It is also helpful to have fun clip art on each word bank page so the students can easily find the desired list. Give each student a folder that holds three-hole punched paper so students can collect the lists for handy reference. Continue to add to the class word books throughout the school year.

Interest Inventory

At the beginning of the school year, have your students complete an Interest Inventory with their parents. This will provide your students with some great writing topics to use throughout the school year. It is very important for young writers to write about things that they know and that are important to them, so what better way than writing about themselves? There is an example of an Interest Inventory on pages 10–11.

My Interest Inventory

1. My full name is Ian Michael Quinn.

2. My nickname is Ian.

3. My birthday is January 7.

4. My favorite meal is pizza and pop.

My Interest Inventory

1. My full name is _____.

2. My nickname is _____.

3. My birthday is _____.

4. My favorite meal is _____.

5. I like to play _____.

6. My favorite TV show is _____.

7. My favorite book is _____.

8. My favorite movie is _____.

9. My favorite type of music is _____.

10. My favorite activity at school is _____.

11. My favorite thing at home is _____.

12. Foods I will not eat are _____.

13. I absolutely hate to _____.

14. My favorite game is _____.

15. I collect _____.

Interest Inventory (cont.)

16. I wish I had a _____ .

17. My most prized possession is _____ .

18. The most important person/people in my life is/are _____

_____ .

19. Things that make me special are _____ .

20. I like to spend my time _____ .

_____ .

21. I'm good at _____ .

22. Something I know about is _____ .

23. Places I have traveled to are _____ .

24. The names of my family members are _____ .

_____ .

25 When I grow up, I want to _____ .

26. Something I would really like to do that I haven't done yet is

_____ .

27. If I could meet anyone in the world, I would like to meet

_____ .

Steps in a Process

Directions: Use the numbered boxes to write the directions for each step in the order of how to complete a task. Draw a picture to go with each direction.

Brainstorming	Directions/Steps in a Process

How to _____

1.

2.

3.

4.

5.

6.

7.

8.

9.

Story Planner

Characters, Setting, Beginning, Middle, End

Directions: Organize a story by writing the characters and setting. At the bottom of the page, draw a picture for what happens at the beginning, in the middle, and at the end of the story.

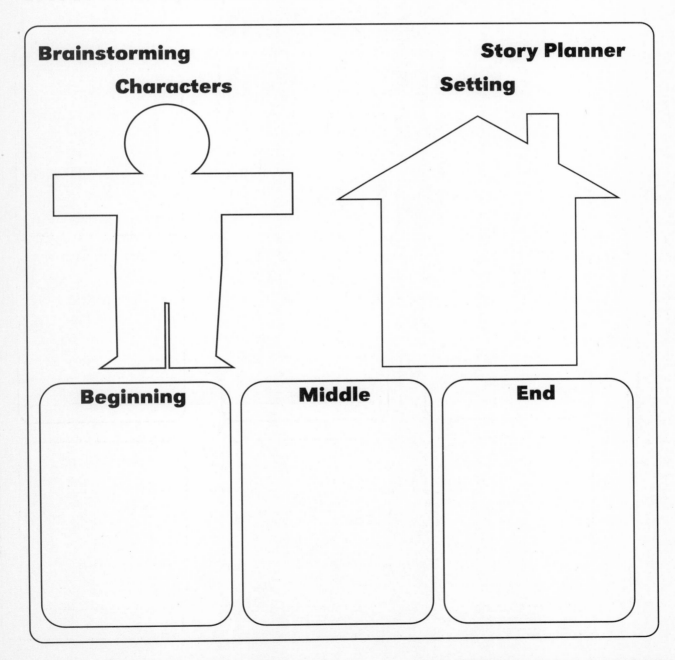

Brainstorming

Characters

Story Planner

Setting

Beginning

Middle

End

Person Writing

Directions: Write details about a person you will be writing about in the balloons.

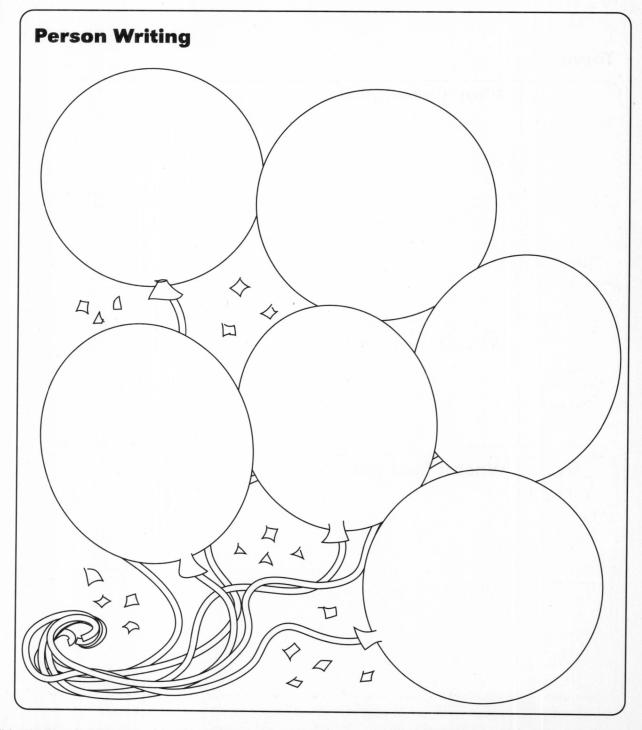

Person Writing

Using the Five Senses

Directions: Use this organizer to write about your senses.

Topic: _____

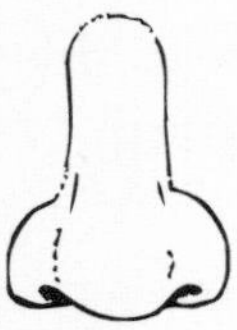

What it smells like
_____
_____
_____

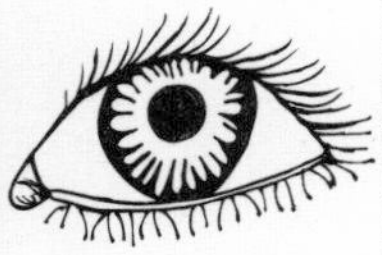

What it looks like
_____
_____
_____

What it tastes like
_____
_____
_____

What it feels like
_____
_____
_____

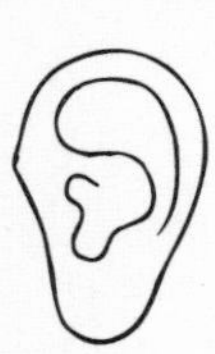

What it sounds like
_____
_____
_____

Monthly Projects

The writing projects in this book incorporate all five writing processes. Below is an overview of the monthly projects.

September Project Overview

Title: All About Me

Final Product: Flap Book

Description: The students will share several things about themselves through this fun project. They will organize their information in a web and then take their writing through the whole process.

Reproducibles Needed:

- All About Me Web (page 21)
- All About Me Writing Sheet (page 40)
- All About Me Clean Copy (page 65)
- All About Me Editing Guide (page 95)
- All About Me Publishing Directions (page 119)

October Project Overview

Title: Letter from America

Final Product: Postcard

Description: The students will write a postcard to a family member as if they have traveled to the new world. (The theme is exploration.) They will organize their information in a list. They will take their writing through the whole process.

Reproducibles Needed:
- Letter from America List (page 22)
- Letter from America Writing Sheet (page 41)
- Letter from America Clean Copy (page 66)
- Letter from America Editing Guide (page 96)
- Letter from America Publishing Directions (page 120)
- Letter from America Postcard Reproducible (page 121)

November Project Overview

Title: Turkey Troubles

Final Product: Puppet Book

Description: The students will write a story from the perspective of a turkey before Thanksgiving and describe what they would do to avoid being on someone's table. They will organize their information on a sequence sheet and take their writing through the whole process.

Reproducibles Needed:

- Turkey Troubles Sequence (page 23)
- Turkey Troubles Writing Sheet (page 42)
- Turkey Troubles Clean Copy (page 67)
- Turkey Troubles Editing Guide (page 97)
- Turkey Troubles Publishing Directions (page 122)
- Turkey Troubles Writing Pages Reproducible (page 123)

December Project Overview

Title: December Celebrations

Final Product: Comparison Book

Description: The students will write how one December celebration (Christmas, Hanukkah, Kwanzaa, St. Lucia's Day, Old Befana, etc.) is different from another. They will share how the two celebrations are alike. They will organize their information in a compare/contrast diagram. They will take their writing through the whole process.

Reproducibles Needed:

- December Celebrations Comparison (page 24)
- December Celebrations Writing Sheet (page 43)
- December Celebrations Clean Copy (page 68)
- December Celebrations Editing Guide (page 98)
- December Celebrations Publishing Directions (page 124)
- December Celebrations Writing Pages Reproducible (page 125)

January Project Overview

Title: Radical Resolutions

Final Product: Sentence Strip Book

Description: Students will write some resolutions for the new year. They will organize their information on a T-chart. They will take their writing through the whole process.

Reproducibles Needed:

- Radical Resolutions T-Chart (page 25)
- Radical Resolutions Writing Sheet (page 44)
- Radical Resolutions Clean Copy (page 69)
- Radical Resolutions Editing Guide (page 99)
- Radical Resolutions Publishing Directions (page 126)

February Project Overview

Title: What I Love Most

Final Product: Shape Book

Description: Students will write things and people they love most in honor of Valentine's Day. They will organize their information in a topic tree and then take their writing through the whole process.

Reproducibles Needed:

- What I Love Most Topic Tree (page 26)
- What I Love Most Writing Sheet (page 45)
- What I Love Most Clean Copy (page 70)
- What I Love Most Editing Guide (page 100)
- What I Love Most Publishing Directions (page 127)
- What I Love Most Heart Shape Reproducible (page 128)

Monthly Projects (cont.)

March Project Overview

Title: Peek-a-Boo Animals

Final Product: Peek-over Book

Description: Students will write facts about an animal of their choice. They will organize their information on a topic tic-tac-toe and then take their writing through the whole process.

Reproducibles Needed:

- Peek-a-Boo Animals Topic Tic-Tac-Toe (page 27)
- Peek-a-Boo Animals Writing Sheet (page 46)
- Peek-a-Boo Animals Clean Copy (page 71)
- Peek-a-Boo Animals Editing Guide (page 101)
- Peek-a-Boo Animals Publishing Directions (page 129)

April Project Overview

Title: Save Our Earth

Final Product: Poster

Description: First-grade students will make a poster to encourage others to take care of our environment in honor of Earth Day. They will organize their information in a Take a Stand web. They will take their writing through the whole process.

Reproducibles Needed:

- Save Our Earth Take a Stand (page 28)
- Save Our Earth Writing Sheet (page 47)
- Save Our Earth Clean Copy (page 72)
- Save Our Earth Editing Guide (page 102)
- Save Our Earth Publishing Directions (page 130)
- Save Our Earth Writing Sections Reproducible (page 131)

May Project Overview

Title: Magnificent Mother

Final Product: Pop-up Book

Description: Students will make a book in honor of their mother or other nurturing role model for Mother's Day. They will organize their information in a person organizer. They will take their writing through the whole process.

Reproducibles Needed:

- Magnificent Mother Person Information (page 29)
- Magnificent Mother Writing Sheet (page 48)
- Magnificent Mother Clean Copy (page 73)
- Magnificent Mother Editing Guide (page 103)
- Magnificent Mother Publishing Directions (page 132)
- Magnificent Mother Pop-up Page Reproducible (page 133)

June Project Overview

Title: Fantastic Father

Final Product: Character Book

Description: Students will make a character book in honor of their father or other nurturing role model for Father's Day. They will organize their information in a person organizer. They will take their writing through the whole process.

Reproducibles Needed:

- Fantastic Father Person Information (page 30)
- Fantastic Father Writing Sheet (page 49)
- Fantastic Father Clean Copy (page 74)
- Fantastic Father Editing Guide (page 104)
- Fantastic Father Publishing Directions (page 134)
- Fantastic Father Writing Page Reproducible (page 135)

September Web

All About Me

Directions: Write your topic in the center and add details about the topic in the boxes.

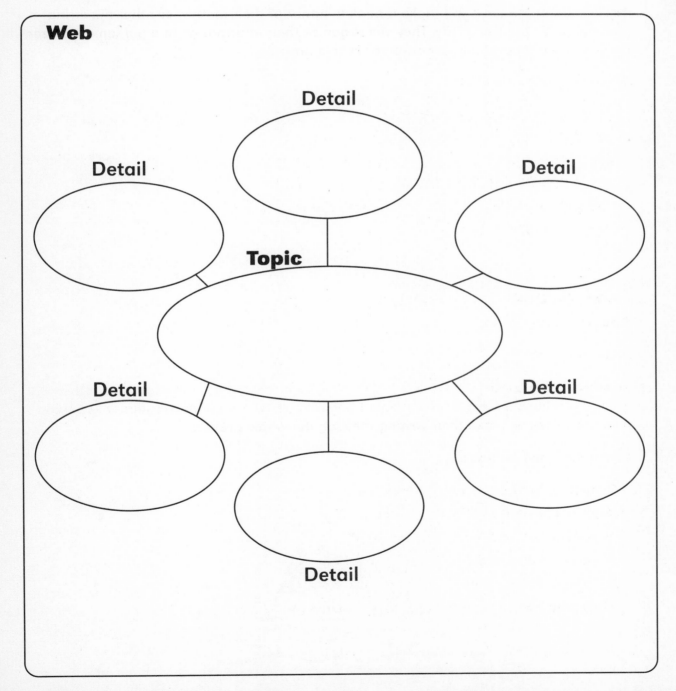

Web

Detail

Detail

Detail

Topic

Detail

Detail

Detail

October List

Letter from America

List

A list about _____

1. _____
   _____

2. _____
   _____

3. _____
   _____

4. _____
   _____

5. _____
   _____

November Sequence

Turkey Troubles

Directions: Write the events in the order that they will occur.

Sequence

First _____

_____

_____

Next _____

_____

_____

Then _____

_____

_____

Last _____

_____

_____

December Comparison

December Celebrations

Directions: Write the two celebrations you are comparing on the lines at the top. In the diamond below Celebration 1, write how it is different from Celebration 2. Follow the same instructions for the second celebration. Write how the celebrations are alike in the middle diamonds.

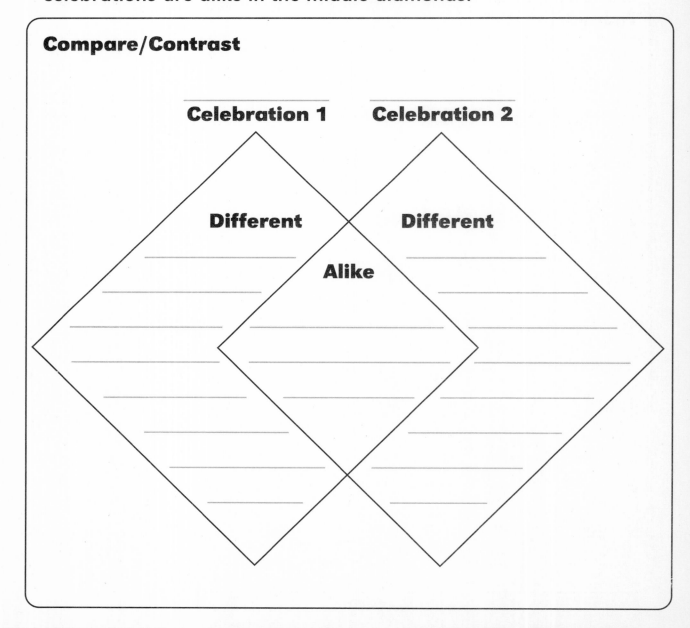

Compare/Contrast

Celebration 1   Celebration 2

Different   Different

Alike

January T-Chart

Radical Resolutions

Directions: On this T-chart, you will write what you have done on the left side and then what you will do on the right side.

T-chart

Last Year	Last Year
1.	1.
2.	2.
3.	3.
4.	4.
5.	5.

February Topic Tree

What I Love Most

Directions: Write what you love most on the trunk of the tree, examples on the large branches, and supporting reasons on the smaller branches.

Topic Tree

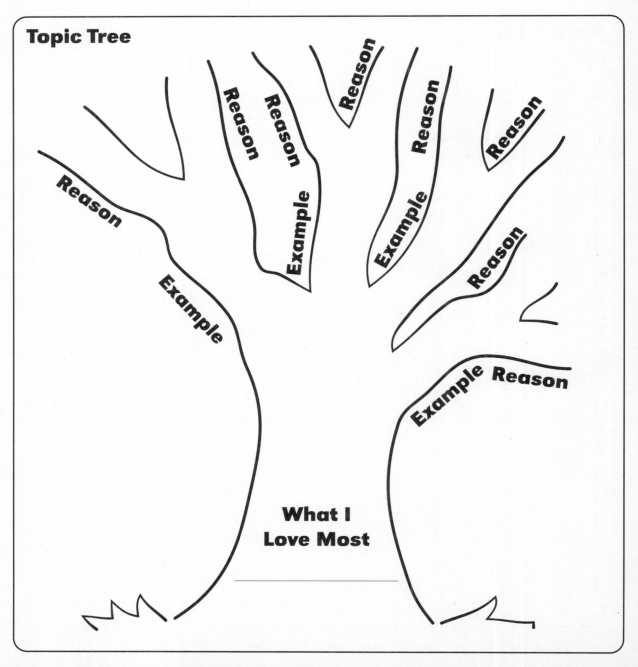

Reason

Reason

Reason

Reason

Reason

Reason

Reason

Reason

Reason

Example

Example

Example

Example Reason

What I Love Most

0-7682-3101-9 *Writing: Total Solutions for Teachers*

March Tic-Tac-Toe

Peek-a-Boo Animals

Directions: Write your animal in the center square. Add supporting details about your animal in the surrounding squares.

Tic-Tac-Toe

	Animal	

April Take a Stand

Save Our Earth

Directions: Write your position about saving our earth in the center circle. Write your reasons why we need to save the earth in the surrounding boxes.

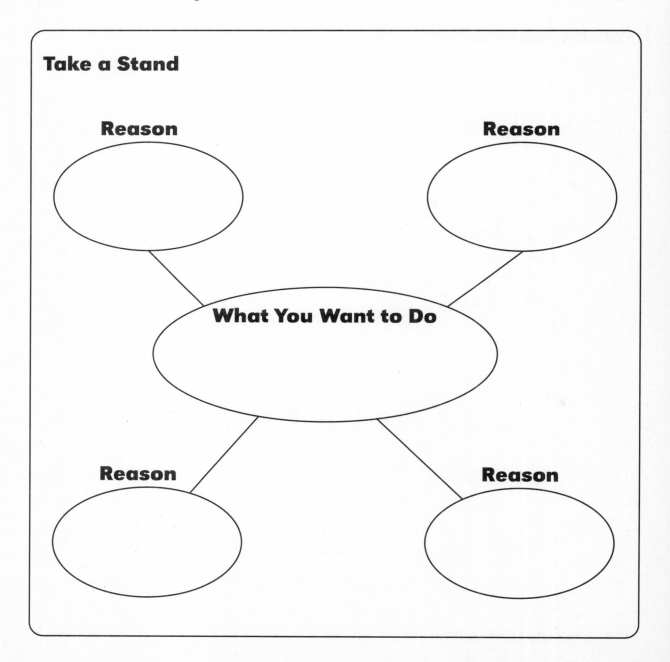

Take a Stand

Reason

Reason

What You Want to Do

Reason

Reason

Magnificent Mother

Directions: On the belt, write the name of the person you are writing about. In each body section, add details about the person.

Person Information

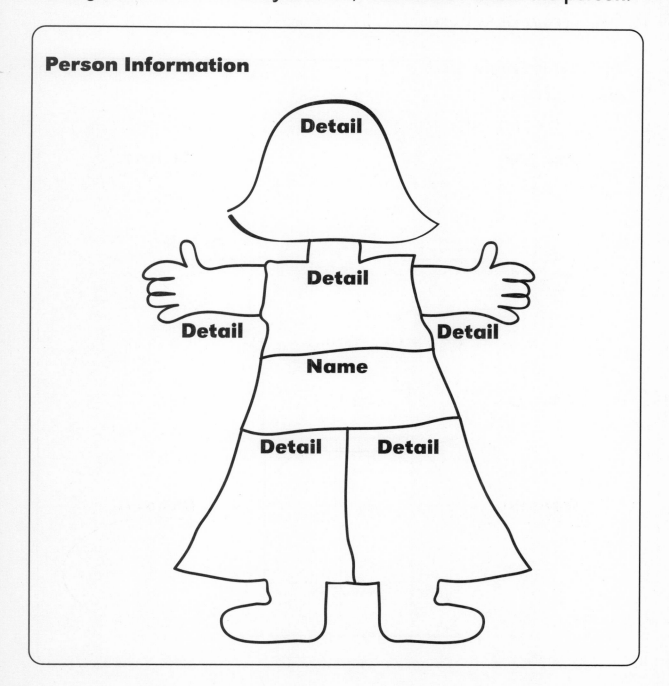

Fantastic Father

Directions: On the belt, write the name of the person you are writing about. In each body section, add details about the person.

Person Information

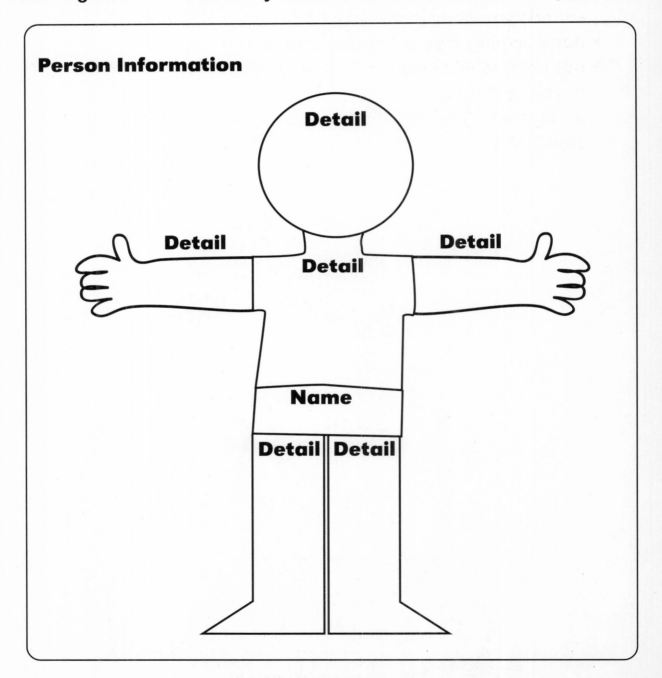

What Is a First Draft?

A First Draft Is...

- getting your ideas down on paper.
- not worrying about the spelling—just writing the sounds you hear in the words.
- not worrying if your handwriting is perfect.
- not erasing—just cross out things you don't want in your writing.
- writing until you have said all you want to say about your topic.

First Draft

First-grade students will think their first draft is their only draft. After some practice, they will learn that the first draft is the second step in the process of going from brainstorming notes to the polished final product.

What You Say, You Can Write!

It is important for you to model this saying to your students. When you give directions, write them on the board after you say them. As you are explaining what you will be doing that day, write a list of daily activities. Let the students observe you writing notes to parents or co-workers. Any examples of writing instead of speaking are excellent models of this idea.

"Talk-Through" Writing

This is similar to "talk-through" brainstorming, but now you are taking your notes and writing the thoughts down on paper in a fairly organized way. It is important to talk as you write—verbalize what you are thinking and what you are doing. This has become second nature for you, but first-grade students have little or no experience with this step. If they continue to hear how you are doing it, they will begin to imitate your strategies.

First Draft (cont.)

Older Student Buddies

Older students have had much more practice with writing and the writing process. It serves two purposes to have older students help younger writers get their ideas down on paper—the young students get to work with someone different, and the older students strengthen their knowledge of the process through teaching. Pair your students with writing buddies. Let the older students give one-on-one assistance to the first-grade students as they go from brainstorming to first draft.

"I'm Stuck!"

A common feeling for first-grade writers is that they don't know how to spell all the words. For many students, it is extremely important to know how to spell the words they are using in their writing. When they get stuck, they look to you for help because you "know all the words." Teach them that you really don't know all the words by "getting stuck" on purpose in your modeled writing. Get the students involved as you try to sound out the unknown word. If they see that it is acceptable in a first draft to just write the sounds they hear in the word, their writing will begin to flow more smoothly.

First Draft (cont.)

When writing a first draft, certain writing strategies will make the whole process easier for you and your students. A few suggestions are

- **Write on Every Other Line**
  The main reason for writing on every other line is to give the students, their peers, and you room to add suggestions or changes in the revision and editing stages. The easiest way to do this is by making an X on every other line. That will remind the students to write only on the lines that have an X.

- **Write on Only One Side of the Paper**
  When the first draft is finished, the students will begin the revision stage. Many times during the revision stage, the paper will be cut apart and reassembled in another way. This will cause problems if writing is on both sides of the sheet.

- **Cross Out Notes as You Write**
  The strategy of crossing out the notes that have been written in a first draft helps to keep writers on track. It also keeps them motivated to continue writing.

There are some great activities to give your students experience with writing a first draft. They include

Season Writing

The following four practice pages will allow the students to practice writing from four provided lists. After selecting your topic, be sure to read through the list with the students and let them share with a partner what they will be writing about.

Writer's Checklist

On page 39, there is a general writer's checklist for students to use when they are finished with their first draft. This provides some guidance to the students as they learn what writing a first draft is all about!

Fall

Directions: Write what you know about the season of fall.

Fall

Word Bank

September, October, November, leaves, red, yellow, brown, orange, football, Halloween, trick-or-treating, costumes, pumpkins, jack-o-lanterns, candy, party, bats, spiders, school, apples, Johnny Appleseed, Fire Safety Week, hay rides, Columbus Day, Thanksgiving, Native Americans, Pilgrim, harvest, feast

Drafting

Directions: Write what you know about the season of winter.

Word Bank

December, January, February, snow, ice, snowballs, snowman, hot chocolate, ice skating, hockey, basketball, Christmas, stockings, Santa, reindeer, elves, candy canes, gingerbread cookies, tree, ornaments, lights, wreaths, Hanukkah, menorah, dreidel, candles, Kwanzaa, Chinese New Year, New Year's Day, Groundhog's Day, Valentine's Day, Presidents' Day, Martin Luther King, Jr. Day

Spring

Directions: Write what you know about the season of spring.

Word Bank

March, April, May, flowers, rain, umbrellas, puddles, baby animals, Easter, Seder, Passover, bunnies, eggs, baskets, birds, vacations, baseball, soccer, St. Patrick's Day, shamrocks, rainbows, pot of gold, leprechauns, lion, lamb, Cinco de Mayo

Drafting

Directions: Write what you know about the season of summer.

Word Bank

June, July, August, sun, warm, beach, sand, castles, lake, ocean, swimming, parks, picnics, bugs, no school, vacation, Fourth of July, fireworks, camping, campfire, marshmallows, lemonade, baseball, boating, sprinklers, fire hydrants, music festivals, block parties, art fairs, carnivals

Writer's Checklist

Writer's Checklist

Name _____

Topic: _____

☐ I have my name on all of the pages.

☐ I have the date on all of the pages.

☐ I wrote everything I know about my topic.

I like this writing because _____

_____

Writer's Checklist

Name _____

Topic: _____

☐ I have my name on all of the pages.

☐ I have the date on all of the pages.

☐ I wrote everything I know about my topic.

I like this writing because _____

_____

All About Me

Directions: Take the information from the brainstorming web on page 21 and write what you will put under each flap. Be sure to write only on the lines that have an X.

Drafting

Flap 1 X _____
X _____

Flap 2 X _____
X _____

Flap 3 X _____
X _____

Flap 4 X _____
X _____

Flap 5 X _____
X _____

October Writing Sheet

Letter from America

Directions: Imagine that you have traveled with an explorer to the new world. Write a letter home to share your experiences on the trip. Be sure to write only on the lines that have an X.

Date: _____

Dear_____ ,

X _____

_____

X _____

_____

X _____

_____

X _____

_____

Sincerely,

_____

November Writing Sheet

Turkey Troubles

Directions: On the feathers, write what happens in your story in order. Be sure to write only on the lines that have an X.

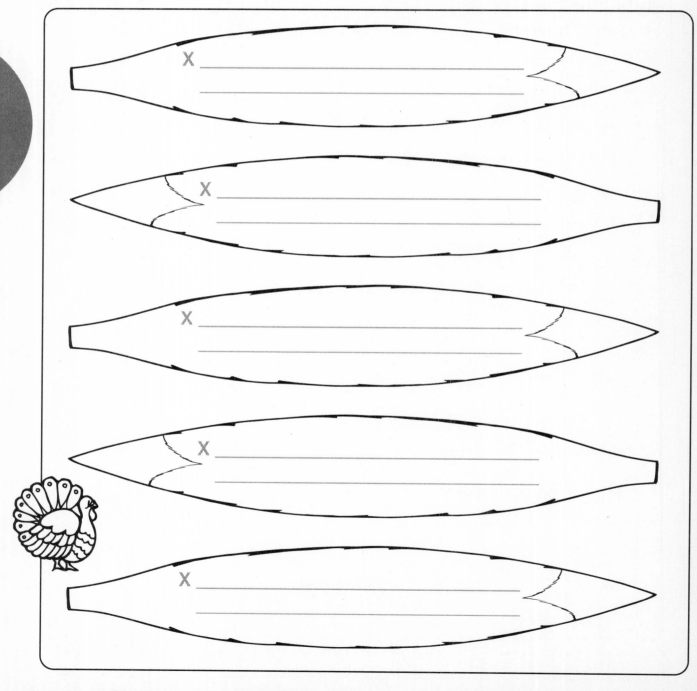

December Writing Sheet

December Celebrations

Directions: Write about the first celebration in the first section and the second celebration in the next section. At the bottom, write how the celebrations are alike. Be sure to write only on the lines that have an X. Use your comparison sheet on page 24 to help you.

Celebration 1: _____

X _____

X _____

Celebration 2: _____

X _____

X _____

How They Are Alike: _____

X _____

X _____

January Writing Sheet

Radical Resolutions

Directions: In each section, write what you will do in the new year. Be sure to write only on the lines that have an X. Use your T-chart from page 25 to help you.

In _____ , I will X _____

X _____

_____

In _____ , I will X _____

X _____

_____

In _____ , I will X _____

X _____

_____

In _____ , I will X _____

X _____

_____

February Writing Sheet

What I Love Most

Directions: In each heart, write about the one thing or person you love the most. Be sure to write only on the lines that have an X. Use your Topic Tree from page 26 to help you.

Drafting

Peek-a-Boo Animals

Directions: In each section, write information about your animal. Be sure to write only on the lines that have an X. Use your Tic Tac Toe Chart from page 27 to help you.

Animal:_____

Page 1	Page 2
X_____	X_____
_____	_____
X_____	X_____
_____	_____

Page 3	Page 4
X_____	X_____
_____	_____
X_____	X_____
_____	_____

Page 5	Page 6
X_____	X_____
_____	_____
X_____	X_____
_____	_____

Page 7	Page 8
X_____	X_____
_____	_____
X_____	X_____
_____	_____

Drafting

April Writing Sheet

Save Our Earth

Directions: In each section, write reasons to support what you want to do to help the earth. Be sure to write only on the lines that have an X. Use your Take a Stand Web from page 28 to help you.

Title: _____

Reason 1

X _____
_____

X _____
_____

X _____
_____

X _____
_____

Reason 2

X _____
_____

X _____
_____

X _____
_____

X _____
_____

Reason 3

X _____
_____

X _____
_____

X _____
_____

X _____
_____

Reason 4

X _____
_____

X _____
_____

X _____
_____

X _____
_____

Magnificent Mother

Directions: Write things about your mother or other important person, for the pop-up book. Be sure to write only on the lines that have an X. Use your person information from page 29.

Drafting

Page 1 X _____

X _____

Page 2 X _____

X _____

Page 3 X _____

X _____

Page 4 X _____

X _____

Page 5 X _____

X _____

Page 6 X _____

X _____

Fantastic Father

Directions: Write things about your father or other important person for the character book. Be sure to write only on the lines that have an X. Use your person information from page 30 to help you.

Page 1 X _____

X _____

Page 2 X _____

X _____

Page 3 X _____

X _____

Page 4 X _____

X _____

Page 5 X _____

X _____

Page 6 X _____

X _____

What Is Revision?

Revision Is...

- deciding what makes sense and what needs more information.
- having others read your writing and helping you improve it.
- cutting apart, moving around, adding information, and taking away things you don't need in your writing.
- adding good five senses words (adjectives).
- praising first, then giving suggestions to make it even better!
- making a clean copy of your writing after you have made your changes.

Revising

Revisions

Typically, first-grade writers see their first drafts as saying exactly what they want them to say. Because it may be difficult for the students to step back and see what they could add or remove, they need a lot of guidance with this process. If they learn it early, however, it will help them continue to grow as writers. Make sure to model the revision process by changing, adding, and removing words and ideas as you write. Also model the revision group process by performing a role-playing skit where you are the writer. Ask for a volunteer to play the role of the teacher.

Three Ways to Revise

1. What words can be replaced or changed?

2. What extra details are not needed and can be removed?

3. What can be added to make it more interesting?

The most important thing to do when revising a piece of writing is to praise first and then give suggestions. In this way, you will encourage the young writers to explore the writing process rather than discourage them. Make sure your writers understand that the Revision Group and the teacher are trying to help make the writing better.

Steps for Revision

- The writer reads the first draft two to three times to self.
- The writing goes to a Revision Group that reads the paper and asks
  - what
  - when
  - where
  - why and
  - how

Questions about the Writing

- The Revision Group completes the response form and attaches it to the writing.
- The teacher reads the writing, completes a response form, and attaches it to the writing.
- The writer meets with the teacher to discuss the suggested revisions.
- The writer revises his or her writing by adding details on the extra lines and crossing out anything he or she want to remove.
- The writer makes a clean copy of the writing with all the changes. On this draft, the writer can write on every line.

Revisions (cont.)

Revising Checklist

Writer's name: _____ Date: _____

Your name: _____ _____

Title: _____

Directions: Use check marks in the blanks.

1. Did the author focus on one idea or topic?

   ☐ yes   ☐ no

2. Is there a clear beginning, middle, and ending?

   ☐ yes   ☐ no

3. Does the title fit the story?

   ☐ yes   ☐ no

4. Does the title get the reader interested?

   ☐ yes   ☐ no

5. What did you have trouble understanding? What was confusing to you?

   _____

   _____

6. What would you like to know more about? _____

   _____

7. What did you like? _____

   _____

Keys to Success with Revision Groups

- The students should be put into groups that will stay the same for the whole school year. This allows the students to build a working relationship as they grow in their abilities to revise their peers' writing.

- There should be only three or four students in each Revision Group. Fewer than three students may not provide enough feedback and more than four likely will be difficult to manage.

- An adult will also be a member of each group. This can be the teacher or a parent volunteer. Young students need a good role model to learn revision, and the adult can act as a guide in the process.

- The papers to be revised should have a number on them, not the writer's name. This allows the students to be unbiased when revising a piece of writing. It also allows the writers to feel comfortable with their peers revising their work.

- It is important that the groups do not get papers from any of the group's members. Each group should help revise students' writing from other groups.

- Read the paper and have the group give feedback. Some guiding questions are

1. What else do you want to know about the writing?
2. Does the writing make sense?
3. Did the writer stay on the topic?
4. Is there anything that doesn't need to be there?
5. Does it make you picture what the writer is describing (five senses words)?

- Complete the Revision Group Response Form on page 55 and staple it to the writing.

Model this process before you start working with revision groups. When the students are initially placed into groups, play a few icebreakers or community- building activities so that group members feel comfortable with each other.

Revising

Revising

Five Senses Words

Adding adjectives (or five senses words) is a great way to make the writing more interesting for the reader. First-grade students are continuing to add to their vocabularies, and it is important to help them create an adjective-rich bank of words to use as they write. You can do this as a class and create posters to display in the classroom for their everyday use. Another suggestion is to use the individual sheets on pages 57–61. The students can record different adjectives on them and keep the sheets in their desks.

Adjective Word Bank

happy

sad

tall

angry

good

pretty

smart

tiny

funny

silly

Revision Practice

A few activities for the students to practice their revising skills are shown on pages 62–64. You can create additional activities to further their experience with revision. Model each step of this process.

Group Response Form

Revision Group Response Forms

Revision Group Name: _____

Date: _____ Paper number: _____

We like this writing because_____

_____

A few of our suggestions are

1. _____

2. _____

3. _____

Revision Group Name: _____

Date: _____ Paper number: _____

We like this writing because_____

_____

A few of our suggestions are

1. _____

2. _____

3. _____

Teacher Response Form

Teacher Response Forms

Writer's Name: _____

Date: _____ Paper number: _____

What I like about your writing is _____

_____

A few of my suggestions are

1. _____

2. _____

3. _____

Writer's Name: _____

Date: _____ Paper number: _____

What I like about your writing is _____

_____

A few of my suggestions are

1. _____

2. _____

3. _____

Touching Words

Revising

Touching Words

Seeing Words

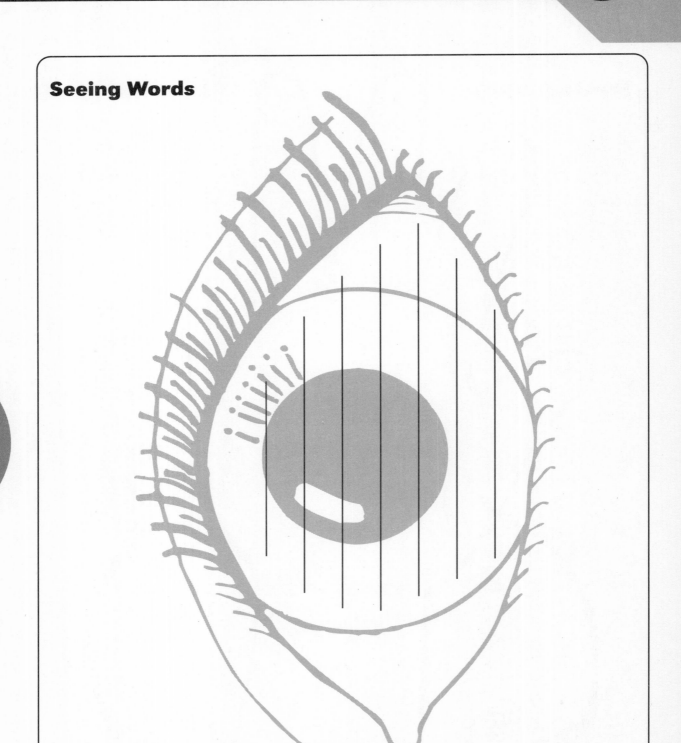

Smelling Words

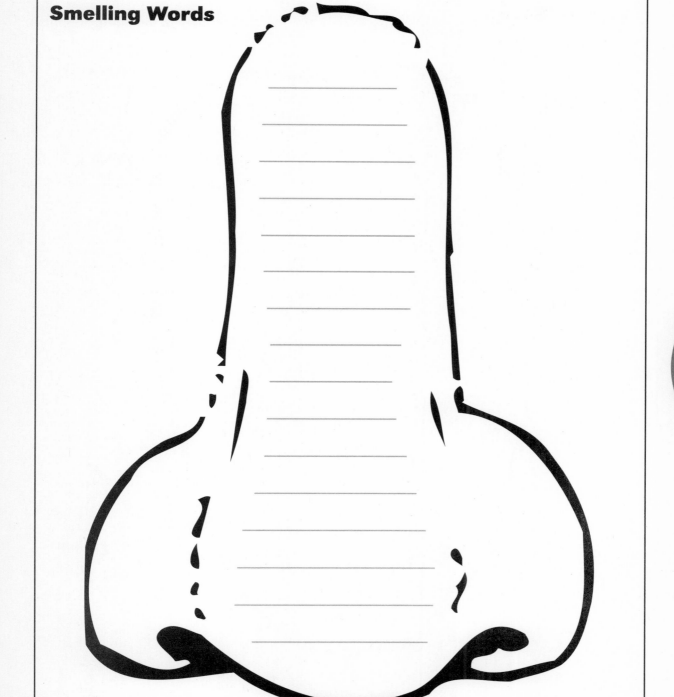

Smelling Words

Tasting Words

Tasting Words

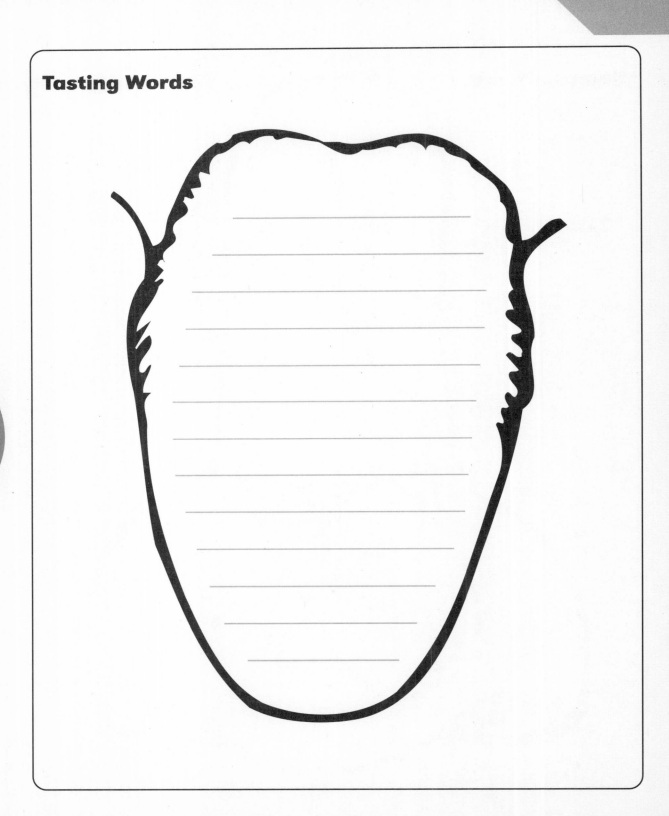

Hearing Words

Hearing Words

Adding More Information

Practice

How to Make a Peanut Butter and Jelly Sandwich

Directions: Add information on the blank lines so the writing makes more sense.

To make a peanut butter and jelly sandwich,

X You need bread.

X Add the peanut butter and

X jelly. Cut the sandwich and

X eat! Yum!

Revising

Rewrite the directions.

To make a peanut butter and jelly sandwich,

X

X

X

X

Removing Extra

Removing Extra Information

Directions: Cross out any information that is not needed in the writing.

A Trip to the Zoo

One sunny day, we went to the zoo. We went in my mom's car.

My mom got her car from my grandma. At the zoo, we saw

lots of animals. The animals were eating, sleeping, and

playing. I like to eat pizza. When we were done at the zoo,

we went for ice cream. What a fun day!

Adding Adjectives

Directions: Add adjectives on the blank lines to make the story more interesting!

A Day at the Beach

It was a _____ day. We got into the _____ car

and were on our way to the beach. Once we got there, we

unpacked the _____ towels, the _____ toys,

and our _____ picnic basket. We found a

_____ spot on the _____ sand. I made a

_____ castle and dug _____ holes in the sand.

The _____ water felt _____ on my feet! It sure

was a _____ day at the beach!

Revising

September Clean Copy

All About Me

Directions: Rewrite your information now that you have made some changes. Draw a practice small picture for each flap.

| Flap 1 _____ | Picture |

| Flap 2 _____ | Picture |

| Flap 3 _____ | Picture |

| Flap 4 _____ | Picture |

| Flap 5 _____ | Picture |

October Clean Copy

Revising

Letter From America

Directions: Rewrite your letter now that you have made some changes.

Date: _____

Dear _____ ,

_____

_____

_____

_____

_____

_____

Sincerely,

_____

Published by Frank Schaffer Publications. Copyright protected. **66** 0-7682-3101-9 *Writing: Total Solutions for Teachers*

Turkey Troubles

Directions: Rewrite your story now that you have made some changes.

Title: _____

Page 1

_____

_____

_____

_____

Page 2

_____

_____

_____

_____

Page 3

_____

_____

_____

_____

Page 4

_____

_____

_____

_____

Revising

December Clean Copy

Directions: Rewrite your comparison now that you have made some changes.

December Celebration:	December Celebration:
_____	_____
1. _____ _____ _____ _____	1. _____ _____ _____ _____
2. _____ _____ _____ _____	2. _____ _____ _____ _____
3. _____ _____ _____ _____	3. _____ _____ _____ _____

Alike:

_____

_____

_____

_____

January Clean Copy

Radical Resolutions

Directions: Rewrite your resolutions now that you have made some changes.

In _____ , I will _____

_____

_____

_____

In _____ , I will _____

_____

_____

_____

In _____ , I will _____

_____

_____

_____

In _____ , I will _____

_____

_____

_____

Revising

February Clean Copy

What I Love Most

Directions: Rewrite your information now that you have made some changes.

What I Love Most

March Clean Copy

Peek-a-Boo Animals

Directions: Rewrite your information about your animal now that you have made some changes.

Animal: _____

Page 1
_____
_____
_____
_____

Page 2
_____
_____
_____
_____

Page 3
_____
_____
_____
_____

Page 4
_____
_____
_____
_____

Page 5
_____
_____
_____
_____

Page 6
_____
_____
_____
_____

Page 7
_____
_____
_____
_____

Page 8
_____
_____
_____
_____

April Clean Copy

Save Our Earth

Directions: Rewrite your information now that you have made some changes.

Topic: _____

Reason 1

_____
_____
_____
_____
_____

Reason 2

_____
_____
_____
_____
_____

Reason 3

_____
_____
_____
_____

Reason 4

_____
_____
_____
_____
_____

Magnificent Mother

Directions: Rewrite your information about your special person now that you have made some changes. Draw a practice picture for each page on another sheet of paper.

Page 1 _____
_____
_____

Page 2 _____
_____
_____

Page 3 _____
_____
_____

Page 4 _____
_____
_____

Page 5 _____
_____
_____

Page 6 _____
_____
_____

Revising

Fantastic Father

Directions: Rewrite your information about your special person now that you have made some changes.

Page 1 _____

Page 2 _____

Page 3 _____

Page 4 _____

Page 5 _____

Page 6 _____

Revising

What Is Editing?

Editing Is...

- making sure capital letters are in the correct place.
- adding punctuation where it is needed.
- correcting misspelled words.
- looking for complete sentences with a "who or what part" and a "what is happening" part.
- the last step before publishing.

Editing

Editing is the making-better step in the writing process. The writing is close to being done; it just needs to be polished before it can become a final project. The polishing includes correcting spelling, capitalization, and punctuation. Because most first-grade students are not competent with these areas in their own writing, it is not recommended to have them edit someone else's work. However, there are a few things they can learn about editing. Here are a few suggestions to get them started:

Word Wall

By incorporating a word wall into your classroom, you are beginning to surround your students with words. Continue to add high-frequency words to your word wall that will be helpful to students in their writing. After you add words to the word wall, require that the students spell those words correctly. Just point to the misspelled word in their writing and tell them that it is on the word wall. Model the words on the word wall often by including them in your writing and speaking throughout the day.

"My Word List"

Some students will want to use words in their writing that may not be common words for the group. In those cases, it is nice to use a "My Word List" to write the words for the students. Each student should have a copy of "My Word List" from pages 82–85 to collect the words he or she wants to use. Then, in the future, the students can refer to the list when they need to spell those words.

Aa
apple
Annie
alligator
alphabet
animal
always
another

0-7682-3101-9 *Writing: Total Solutions for Teachers*

First-Grade Word Bookmarks

These are like mini word walls for the students to use during their writing. The bookmarks are quick, easy, and right at the students' fingertips. Copy the one provided on page 86 onto cardstock paper or create one of your own! Model the bookmarks by using them in your own writing.

Circle Unknown Words

First-grade students are a little too young to start using a dictionary to check their spelling, and you may choose not to introduce dictionaries at this time. Instead of going to a dictionary, they can circle words in their writing that they are unsure about. As long as they are trying to write the words to their best ability, that is all that matters. Remind them that they will continue to learn to spell new words throughout their writing.

All Writers Make Mistakes

One of the most important things to stress with first-grader writers is that all writers make mistakes. There are no mistakes in writing, just changes. Because all writing is a process, no one writes something perfectly the first time. There are always things to be changed or fixed. Making mistakes is how we learn new things, and that applies to writing, too!

> My howse
> My howse
> is in tha
> sittee. I haf
> a tre in frond.

Editing

Daily Oral Language

One way to get daily practice with editing is by using Daily Oral Language. There are different programs available, but you can easily do this on your own. Make up one or two sentences a day to work on a specific editing skill. Model this by writing the sentences on the board or overhead for the students to correct. You can do this as a whole group or individually. These are great as morning warm-up activities!

Wacky News

Another way to give your students editing practice is to write the daily news with some mistakes. The students can then correct the mistakes and rewrite the news. This can also be done as a whole group. As you correct the news, you will be able to share what will happen during the day.

Editing Checklist

On page 80, there is a general editing checklist that can be used with any writing project. The writers complete the checklist after they have finished their editing to make sure they have done all they can do.

Name: _____

Title of writing: _____

☐ My name is on the paper.

☐ I started all my sentences with capital letters.

☐ I ended my sentences with punctuation (! . ?).

I am proud of my writing because _____

0-7682-3101-9 *Writing: Total Solutions for Teachers*

Editing

Editing (cont.)

Buddy Editing Checklist

Even though first-grader are not experienced enough to check all the words for correct spelling, they can learn the process by checking the word wall words in a peer's writing. They can also give their input on capitalization and punctuation. A Buddy Editing Checklist is on page 81. Make an overhead copy of the checklist and review the process with the entire group. Use a piece of writing that you have created or one that belongs to a student in another class or grade as a model for editing.

Teacher's Role in Editing

The following suggestions can assist you as you edit your students' writing.

- Correct papers in front of each student, but do it privately. It will make it more comfortable for the student.

- Explain why the corrections need to be made. This is a wonderful time to give a mini-lesson that is meaningful to the student.

- Reassure students that it is normal to not know how to spell every word—very few people do.

- Praise, praise, praise! For everything that needs to be fixed, there should be a positive thing to say about the writing. At this point in the process, there should be plenty to praise.

Name: Julio

Title of writing: Maria

☑ My name is on the paper.

☑ I started all my sentences with capital letters.

☑ I ended my sentences with punctuation (! . ?).

I am proud of my writing because _I used describing_

words about my abuela.

Editing

Editing Checklist

Editing Checklists

Name:_____

Title of writing:_____

☐ My name is on the paper.

☐ I started all my sentences with capital letters.

☐ I ended my sentences with punctuation (! . ?).

I am proud of my writing because _____

_____

Name:_____

Title of writing:_____

☐ My name is on the paper.

☐ I started all my sentences with capital letters.

☐ I ended my sentences with punctuation (! . ?).

I am proud of my writing because _____

_____

80 0-7682-3101-9 *Writing: Total Solutions for Teachers*

Editing

Buddy Editing Checklist

Buddy Editing Checklists

Editing buddy's name: _____

Writer's name: _____

Title of writing: _____

Did the writer

☐ start sentences with capital letters?

☐ end sentences with punctuation (! . ?)?

☐ use correct spelling of word wall words?

I like this paper because _____

_____

Editing buddy's name: _____

Writer's name: _____

Title of writing: _____

Did the writer

☐ start sentences with capital letters?

☐ end sentences with punctuation (! . ?)?

☐ use correct spelling of word wall words?

I like this paper because _____

_____

Editing

My Word List

Aa

_____
_____
_____
_____
_____
_____

Cc

_____
_____
_____
_____
_____
_____

Ee

_____
_____
_____
_____
_____
_____

Bb

_____
_____
_____
_____
_____
_____

Dd

_____
_____
_____
_____
_____
_____

Ff

_____
_____
_____
_____
_____
_____

My Word List (cont.)

Gg

_____
_____
_____
_____
_____
_____
_____

Ii

_____
_____
_____
_____
_____
_____
_____

Kk

_____
_____
_____
_____
_____
_____
_____

Hh

_____
_____
_____
_____
_____
_____

Jj

_____
_____
_____
_____
_____
_____

Ll

_____
_____
_____
_____
_____
_____

My Word List (cont.)

Mm

_____

_____

_____

_____

_____

_____

_____

Oo

_____

_____

_____

_____

_____

_____

_____

Qq

_____

_____

_____

_____

_____

_____

_____

Nn

_____

_____

_____

_____

_____

_____

_____

Pp

_____

_____

_____

_____

_____

_____

_____

Rr

_____

_____

_____

_____

_____

_____

_____

My Word List (cont.)

Ss

Uu

Ww

Xx

Tt

Vv

Yy

Zz

85 0-7682-3101-9 *Writing: Total Solutions for Teachers*

First-Grade Bookmarks

First-Grade Words Bookmark

a	don't
about	down
after	each
all	find
am	first
an	for
and	from
are	get
as	girl
asked	go
at	going
away	good
back	had
be	has
because	have
been	he
before	her
big	here
boy	him
but	his
by	house
called	how
came	I
can	I am
come	if
could	in
day	into
did	is
do	it

First-Grade Words Bookmark

just	out	us
keep	over	use
kind	people	very
know	play	was
like	put	way
little	ran	we
long	run	went
look	said	were
looked	saw	what
made	see	when
make	she	where
man	so	which
may	some	who
more	than	will
most	that	with
mother	the	would
me	their	you
my	them	your
no	then	
not	there	
now	these	
of	they	
old	this	
on	three	
one	time	
only	to	
or	too	
other	two	
our	up	

Names of People

Directions: Capitalize the names of people. Rewrite the sentences correctly.

1. My friend ben likes to play with me.

_____

_____

2. I went to the zoo with jill.

_____

_____

3. We saw nick at the game.

_____

_____

4. On Monday, mario will go to the store.

_____

_____

5. We will learn about christopher columbus.

_____

_____

Editing

Names of Places

Directions: Capitalize the names of places. Rewrite the sentences correctly.

1. My family ate dinner at jim's crab shack.

_____

_____

2. We went to florida for our vacation.

_____

_____

3. I got a new bat and ball from sports world.

_____

_____

4. The students at west elementary school read a lot of books.

_____

_____

5. My mom went to old town bank to get some money.

_____

_____

Names of Days

Directions: Capitalize the names of days and months. Rewrite the sentences correctly.

1. On monday, we will go to the park.

_____

_____

2. Kim's birthday is in march.

_____

_____

3. We do not have school on saturday or sunday.

_____

_____

4. The summer months are june, july, and august.

_____

_____

5. José will come over on friday to play.

_____

_____

Editing

Periods

. **This punctuation mark is called a peroid.**

Directions: Each sentence below is actually two sentences. Put a period at the end of each sentence. Rewrite the sentences on the lines underneath. Remember to capitalize the beginning of the new sentences.

1. I went to the store I got apples for a pie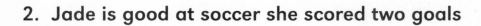

   _____

   _____

2. Jade is good at soccer she scored two goals

   _____

   _____

3. The dog has a bone she will bury it in the yard

   _____

   _____

4. My favorite color is blue I like the color green, too

   _____

   _____

90 0-7682-3101-9 *Writing: Total Solutions for Teachers*

Question Marks

? This punctuation mark is called a question mark.

Directions: Add question marks to the asking sentences. Add periods to the telling sentences.

1. The boy likes to fish

2. Will you take out the trash

3. Did he get a new bike

4. A duck is in the water

5. Can I have some water

6. Sam and Keisha are friends

7. The man is on the bench

8. When will we go to the park

9. We will go to the zoo

10. What is your name

Directions: Circle the first word in the asking sentences. Write each word below. Certain words let you know that a sentence is a question.

_____   _____

_____   _____

_____

Exclamation Points

! This punctuation mark is called an exclamation point.

Directions: Add exclamation points to the sentences that show excitement. Add periods to the telling sentences.

1. Watch out

2. I am going to school

3. There are fish in the pond

4. What a great day

5. Tim wants to ride on the train

6. This is fun

7. My mom works at the library

8. The dog wants to go for a walk

9. Ouch, that hurts

10. We won our game

Adding "ed" to Words

Directions: When you add *ed* to the end of a word, it means something already happened. Choose which word fits best into the sentence.

1. The boy _____ the tree. (climb, climbed)

2. A frog _____ into the pond. (hop, hopped)

3. He will _____ to the store. (skip, skipped)

4. I _____ on the phone last night. (talk, talked)

5. She is going to _____ her homework. (finish, finished)

Directions: Change these words by adding *ed*.

1. walk _____

2. jump_____

3. push_____

4. park _____

5. call_____

Adding "ing" to Words

Directions: When you add *ing* to the end of a word, it means something is happening right now. Choose which word fits best into the sentence.

1. My friend is _____ to me. (talk, talking)

2. I will _____ in the race. (run, running)

3. He is _____ a football. (throw, throwing)

4. They like _____ that game. (play, playing)

5. She will _____ a dress to the party. (wear, wearing)

Directions: Change these words by adding *ing*.

1. crash_____

2. roar_____

3. show_____

4. soar_____

5. see_____

September Editing Guide

All About Me Editing Guides

Name:_____

☐ I started all my sentences with capital letters.

☐ My telling sentences end with a period.

☐ All names start with a capital letter.

☐ I have picture ideas for all the flaps.

I am proud of my All About Me book because _____

_____

Name:_____

☐ I started all my sentences with capital letters.

☐ My telling sentences end with a period.

☐ All names start with a capital letter.

☐ I have picture ideas for all the flaps.

I am proud of my All About Me book because _____

_____

Editing

October Editing Guide

Letter from America Editing Guides

Name:_____

☐ I started all my sentences with capital letters.

☐ My telling sentences end with a period(.) .

☐ My asking sentences end with a question mark (?).

☐ All names, days, and months start with a capital letter.

I am proud of my Letter from America because _____

_____

Name:_____

☐ I started all my sentences with capital letters.

☐ My telling sentences end with a period(.) .

☐ My asking sentences end with a question mark (?).

☐ All names, days, and months start with a capital letter.

I am proud of my Letter from America because _____

_____

Editing

November Editing Guide

Turkey Troubles Editing Guides

Name:_____

☐ All the words in my title start with a capital letter.

☐ I started all my sentences with capital letters.

☐ My telling sentences end with a period(.) .

☐ My asking sentences end with a question mark (?).

☐ My excited sentences end with an exclamation point (!).

I am proud of my Turkey Troubles project because _____

_____

Name:_____

☐ All the words in my title start with a capital letter.

☐ I started all my sentences with capital letters.

☐ My telling sentences end with a period(.) .

☐ My asking sentences end with a question mark (?).

☐ My excited sentences end with an exclamation point (!).

I am proud of my Turkey Troubles project because _____

_____

Editing

December Editing Guide

December Celebrations Editing Guides

Name:_____

☐ I started all my sentences with capital letters.

☐ My telling sentences end with a period(.) .

☐ My excited sentences end with an exclamation point (!).

☐ All holiday names start with a capital letter.

I am proud of my December Celebrations project because

_____

_____

Name:_____

☐ I started all my sentences with capital letters.

☐ My telling sentences end with a period(.) .

☐ My excited sentences end with an exclamation point (!).

☐ All holiday names start with a capital letter.

I am proud of my December Celebrations project because

_____

_____

Editing

January Editing Guide

Radical Resolutions Editing Guides

Name:_____

☐ All my sentences with capital letters.

☐ My telling sentences end with a period(.) .

☐ My excited sentences end with an exclamation point (!).

I am proud of my Radical Resolutions project because

_____

_____

The resolution I plan to keep is _____

Name:_____

☐ All my sentences with capital letters.

☐ My telling sentences end with a period(.) .

☐ My excited sentences end with an exclamation point (!).

I am proud of my Radical Resolutions project because

_____

_____

The resolution I plan to keep is _____

Editing

February Editing Guide

What I Love Most Editing Guides

Name:_____

- ☐ I started all my sentences with capital letters.
- ☐ My telling sentences end with a period(.) .
- ☐ My excited sentences end with an exclamation point (!).
- ☐ All names and places start with an capital letter.

I am proud of my What I Love Most project because

_____

_____

Name:_____

- ☐ I started all my sentences with capital letters.
- ☐ My telling sentences end with a period(.) .
- ☐ My excited sentences end with an exclamation point (!).
- ☐ All names and places start with an capital letter.

I am proud of my What I Love Most project because

_____

_____

Editing

March Editing Guide

Peek-a-Boo Animals Editing Guides

Name:_____

☐ All my sentences with capital letters.

☐ My telling sentences end with a period(.) .

☐ My excited sentences end with an exclamation point (!).

I am proud of my Peek-a-Boo Animals project because

_____

_____

Name:_____

☐ All my sentences with capital letters.

☐ My telling sentences end with a period(.) .

☐ My excited sentences end with an exclamation point (!).

I am proud of my Peek-a-Boo Animals project because

_____

_____

Editing

April Editing Guide

Save Our Earth Editing Guides

Name:_____

☐ All of the words in my title start with a capital letter.

☐ I started all my sentences with capital letters.

☐ My telling sentences end with a period(.) .

☐ My excited sentences end with an exclamation point (!).

I am proud of my Save Our Earth project because

_____

_____

Name:_____

☐ All of the words in my title start with a capital letter.

☐ I started all my sentences with capital letters.

☐ My telling sentences end with a period(.) .

☐ My excited sentences end with an exclamation point (!).

I am proud of my Save Our Earth project because

_____

_____

May Editing Guide

Magnificent Mother Editing Guide

Name:_____

☐ I started all my sentences with capital letters.

☐ My telling sentences end with a period(.) .

☐ My excited sentences end with an exclamation point (!).

☐ All names and places start with a capital letter.

☐ I have pop-up picture idea for all the pages.

I am proud of my Magnificent Mother project because

_____

_____

My mom or special person will like this because _____

_____

_____

Editing

Fantastic Father Editing Guide

Name:_____

☐ I started all my sentences with capital letters.

☐ My telling sentences end with a period(.) .

☐ My excited sentences end with an exclamation point (!).

☐ All names and places start with a capital letter.

I am proud of my Fantastic Father project because

_____

_____

My dad or special person will like this because _____

_____

_____

_____

Editing

What Is Publishing?

Publishing Is...

- a polished copy of your writing.
- a lot more than just putting writing into traditional books.
- finding a fun way to display your writing.
- sharing your work with others (your audience).
- a time to be PROUD of all the hard work you have done!

Publishing

Publishing is the time for students to show off all their hard work! They have done a lot to get to this point and they should be very proud of all the work they have completed during the writing process. When the students begin to feel a sense of accomplishment, they will be more motivated to do it all over again!

There are several ways to model the publishing process. If your school has a publishing center, arrange a trip to visit the center with your class. When the class has finished a writing assignment or has completed a monthly writing project, publish your example by reading it to the class. Organize a writer's fair where members of the community are the audience. Show a video, television show like *Reading Rainbow* on PBS, or a filmstrip or movie on a published author like Ezra Jack Keats or Eric Carle. The experience is the ultimate modeling of the publishing process.

Publishing can include

- reading your work out loud.
- adding your work to a class book.
- making a book by only you.
- doing a variety of different projects to display your writing!

When publishing, there are a few things to remember

- Write neatly or type on a computer.
- Take your time.
- Do your best work!

106 0-7682-3101-9 *Writing: Total Solutions for Teachers*

Publishing

Since publishing is the final stage of the writing process and most of the work is finished, it is time to have some fun! Here are a few suggestions for getting the students excited about publishing their writing.

Spotlight on Writers

Designate an area in your classroom to hang published work by the students. This allows others to enjoy the writing projects, too. It also gives the writers a sense of pride to see their hard work displayed for all to see!

Author Visits

Talk with other teachers and set up a time to have your students visit their classrooms to share their writing projects. The more the writers get to share their work, the better they will understand the purpose for writing.

Writing Buddies

Set up a buddy system with an older class or a senior citizens group, where partners work on a writing project together. The finished projects can be published by creating an electronic catalog of "great works" on videotape.

Review Circle

Have the students give their positive feedback on the published work—like movie or book reviewers! It is rewarding for the writers to hear how others enjoyed their writing.

Writing Open House

Toward the end of the school year, have an evening for parents to come to your classroom and see all the writing projects the students have completed. Have the students write their invitations for this event. The parents will be delighted to see how much their children have grown in their learning over the year!

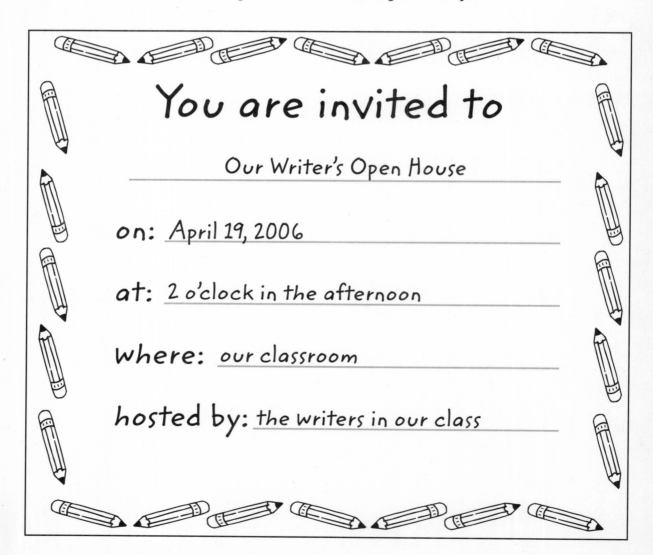

You are invited to

Our Writer's Open House

on: April 19, 2006

at: 2 o'clock in the afternoon

where: our classroom

hosted by: the writers in our class

108

Publishing

September Stationery

October Stationery

Practice

Publishing

November Stationery

December Stationery

January Stationery

February Stationery

March Stationery

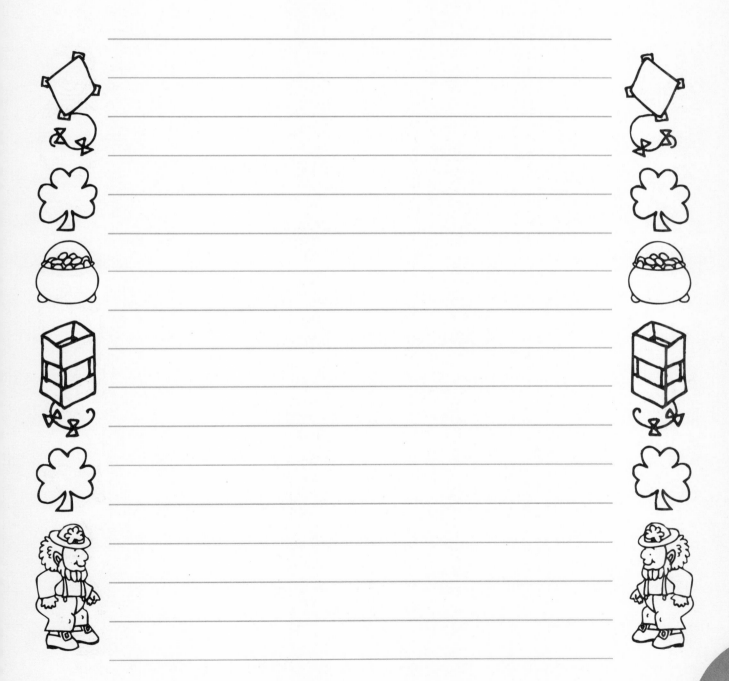

April Stationery

May Stationery

June Stationery

All About Me

Publishing Directions

Materials:

- 9" x 12" construction paper in a light color
- scissors
- crayons
- pencils

Directions:

1. Take the construction paper and fold it in half the long way.

2. Cut one side to the middle to make five flaps (the back part should not be cut).

3. Draw the pictures on top of the flaps and write the corresponding information under each flap.

Optional:

You could do the writing on small pieces of paper that fit inside the flaps. Glue them into place.

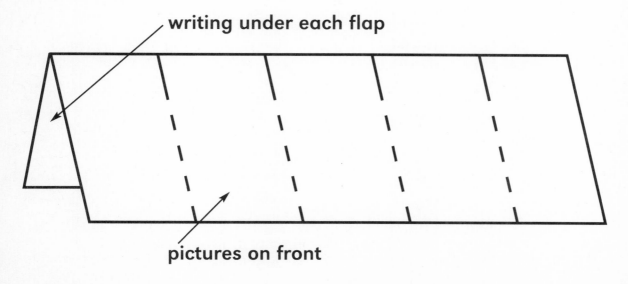

writing under each flap

pictures on front

Letter from America

Publishing Directions

Materials:

- postcard reproducible (page 121 copied on cardstock paper)
- scissors
- crayons
- pencils

Directions:

1. Cut out the postcard from page 121.

2. On the back, draw a picture of what one of the lands in the new world looked like.

3. On the front, write the name and address of one of your family members. Decorate the stamp on the right side of the postcard. Write your letter on the left half.

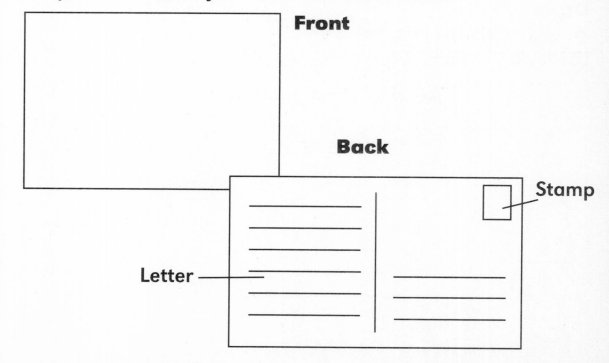

Front

Back

Stamp

Letter

Postcard

Letter from America

Turkey Trouble

Publishing Directions

Materials:
- brown lunch bags
- construction paper
- writing page reproducible (page 123)
- scissors
- glue
- stapler
- pencils

Directions:
1. Use the construction paper to make a turkey.

2. Glue the turkey onto the bottom of the lunch bag.

3. Write the story from the writing pages on page 123.

4. Cut out the writing pages. Staple them to the back of the lunch bag under the turkey.

5. Write the title above the stapled pages.

6. When you put your hand in the turkey puppet book, the turkey should move up and down.

122   0-7682-3101-9 *Writing: Total Solutions for Teachers*

Turkey Trouble (cont.)

Turkey Trouble Writing Pages

December Celebrations

Publishing Directions

Materials:
- light-colored construction paper (8" x 8")
- writing page reproducible (page 125)
- scissors
- stapler
- pencils

Directions:
1. Write the information about each December Celebration from the writing pages on page 125.

2. Cut out the writing pages and stack them in order.

3. Staple them at the top of the pages, side by side on the light construction paper.

4. Write how the celebrations are alike behind the stapled pages on the construction paper.

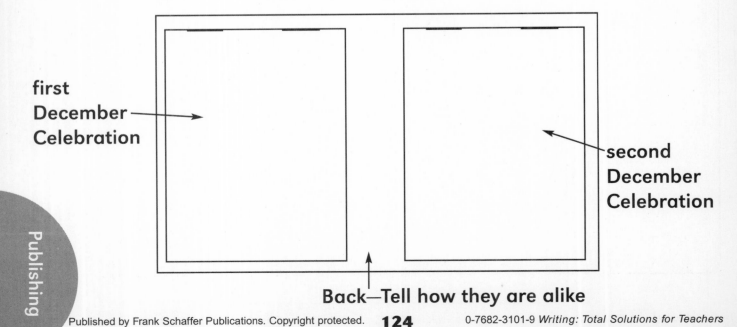

first December Celebration

second December Celebration

Back—Tell how they are alike

December Celebrations Writing Pages

December Celebration:

December Celebration:

Radical Resolutions

Publishing Directions

Materials:
- cardstock sentence strips (one per book)
- 3" x 11" strips of white paper (writing pages)
- scissors
- stapler
- markers
- pencils

Directions:
1. Staple strips of white paper to the right side of the sentence strip.

2. On the sentence strip, write "In _____, I will."
   (insert year)

3. Trace over your writing with a marker.

4. On the writing pages, write your resolutions.

In _____ , I will

What I Love Most

Publishing Directions

Materials:

- heart-shape reproducible (page 128)
- pink, red, or purple construction paper
- scissors
- small hole punch
- brass fastener or yarn
- pencils

Directions:

1. Write the information from the heart-shaped writing pages on page 128.

2. Cut out the heart pages.

3. Trace one of the heart pages onto construction paper.

4. Put another piece of construction paper underneath and cut out the heart shape from both pieces of paper.

5. On the front cover, write "What I Love Most."

6. Use a small hole punch to punch a small hole in the bottom of each heart.

7. Secure the pages with a brass fastener or piece of yarn.

What I Love Most Heart Shape

0-7682-3101-9 *Writing: Total Solutions for Teachers*

Peek-a-Boo Animals

Publishing Directions

Materials:

- construction paper (9" x 12")
- white paper (8.5" x 11")
- scissors
- glue
- stapler
- pencils

Directions:

1. Stack four pieces of white paper and fold them in half the long way (so they become 4.25" x 11").

2. Fold a piece of construction paper in half the long way.

3. Put the folded white paper inside the folded construction paper and staple at the top.

4. Use construction paper to make a head and paws of your animal.

5. Glue the paws and head onto the cover of the book (along the folded edge) so it looks like the animal is peeking over.

6. Write the name of the animal on the front cover.

7. On the white pages, write the animal information.

Save Our Earth

Publishing Directions

Materials:
- poster board
- writing page reproducible (page 131)
- scissors
- glue
- markers
- pencils

Directions:

1. Write the information from the writing pages on page 131.

2. Cut out the writing pages and glue them onto the poster near the four corners.

3. Write the title in the middle. Draw pictures to illustrate your position.

4. Color with markers.

picture of Earth

writing pieces

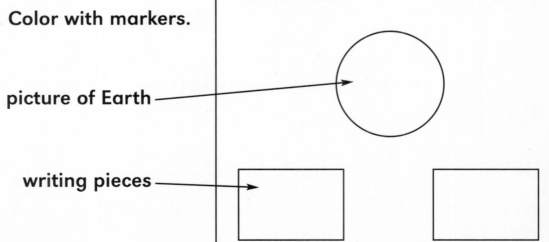

 0-7682-3101-9 *Writing: Total Solutions for Teachers*

Publishing

Save Our Earth (cont.)

Save Our Earth Writing Pages

Magnificent Mother

Materials:

- construction paper (6" x 9")
- scrap construction paper
- pop-up page reproducible (page 133)
- scissors
- glue
- stapler
- markers
- pencils

Directions:

1. Write the information from your writing sheet on the pop-up pages.

2. Cut out the pages and fold on the line.

3. Cut on the two lines in the middle. Fold the pop-up in the opposite direction of the paper fold so it sticks out from the page.

4. Fold the construction paper in half and staple the top of the first page to the construction paper.

5. Staple the top of the second page to the bottom back of the first page. Continue with the remaining pages.

6. Staple the bottom of the last page to the construction paper.

7. As you open each page, the middle should pop up.

8. Use the scrap construction paper to make the pictures that pop-up on each page.

Magnificent Mother Pop-up Page

Fantastic Father

Materials:
- construction paper (12" x 18")
- writing page reproducible (page 135)
- additional construction paper
- scissors
- glue
- stapler
- tape
- pencils

staple the writing pages (inside)

cut-off pieces

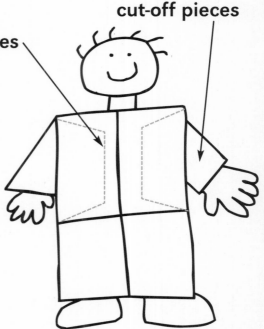

Directions:

1. Fold the construction paper until you have eight equal sections (see picture).

2. Cut the bottom corner sections off. Save these sections.

3. Fold the top corner section in like a vest.

4. Tape the saved sections onto the back so they stick out as arms.

5. Add details to make a person by adding construction paper features like a head, neck, hands, and feet.

6. Write the information from the writing pages on page 135.

7. Cut out the writing pages and staple them in order inside the vest (on the body).

134 0-7682-3101-9 *Writing: Total Solutions for Teachers*

Fantastic Father (cont.)

Fantastic Father Writing Pages

Class Book Topics

There are endless ideas to write about when making a class book. Here are just a few to get you started.

1. When I was little...

2. When I grow up...

3. I am happy when...

4. It makes me sad when...

5. My favorite memory is...

6. If I were one inch tall...

7. If I lived at the zoo...

8. A visit from an alien

9. Being a good friend means...

10. I want...

11. I need...

12. At school, I like to...

13. The ultimate birthday party

14. If I could fly...

15. I get the giggles when...

16. If I were the president...

17. What the world needs

18. With my magic glasses, I can see...

19. My favorite time of the day...

20. At recess, I like to...

21. I am responsible for...

22. I wish...

23. If I were a cartoon character...

24. If I met _____ (famous person)...

25. The best thing about being in first grade is... (This one is great to save and read to the next year's class during the first week!)

ABC Book List

ABC books are fun to read to your students, but they are also great examples of different ways you could make ABC books as a class. Here are a few.

A My Name Is... by Alice Lyne
- This is a fun book that deals with different names and different cultures. It is a great book for learning about similarities and differences among people.

The Letters Are Lost by Lisa Campbell Ernst
- The alphabet wooden blocks are lost around the house! This book goes on a hunt to find the letters in some pretty strange locations.

Alphabeep—A Zipping, Zooming ABC by Debora Pearson
- Have you ever played an alphabet game on a road trip? This fun book finds things on the road for all the letters of the alphabet.

Naughty Little Monkeys by Jim Aylesworth
- A very cute book written by a former first-grade teacher. The monkeys are naughty but very funny.

K Is for Kissing a Cool Kangaroo by Giles Andreae and Guy Parker-Rees
- This fun, rhyming book has great illustrations that go from A to Z.

Z Goes Home by Jon Agee
- The letter Z leaves his job at the city zoo and heads home. Z sees many interesting things on his journey home!

Writing Book List

The Way I Feel by Janan Cain
- Choose an emotion from the book and write when you feel that way.

Friends by Helme Heine
- Write what it takes to be a good friend.

Dear Mrs. LaRue: Letters from Obedience School by Mark Teague
- This book provides a good model for letter writing.

Sometimes I'm Bombaloo by Rachel Vail
- Write about what it feels like when you get really mad.

Ella Sarah Gets Dressed by Margaret Chodos-Irvine
- Describe your favorite outfit.

The Recess Queen by Alexis O'Neill and Laura Huliska-Beith
- Write about how you would deal with someone who is being mean to you.
- Also good for bright and inventive language.

The Brand New Kid by Katherine Couric
- Tell how you would welcome a new kid to your school.

Armadillo Tattletale by Helen Ketteman and Keith Graves
- Explain why it is important to not be a tattletale.

George Shrinks by William Joyce
- Write about the adventures you would take if you were as small as George.

138   0-7682-3101-9 *Writing: Total Solutions for Teachers*

Writing Book List (cont.)

If I Had a Robot by Dan Yaccarino
- Tell what you would have your own personal robot do for you!

Stand Tall, Molly Lou Melon by Patty Lovell and Davis Catrow
- Describe the things about you that make you special and unique.

Oliver Button is a Sissy by Tomi dePaola
- What makes you different from other people?

Tuesday by David Wiesner
- Write the words to go with the fun pictures in this book.

How I Spent My Summer Vacation by Mark Teague
- Tell about your adventures from summer vacation.

Me First by Helen Lester
- Explain why it isn't always best to be first.

The Little Scarecrow Boy by Margaret Wise Brown
- Describe something that you want to do now but have to wait until you are older to do.

Sweet Dream Pie by Audrey Wood
- Describe your perfect pie.
- Write about a funny dream.

The Flying Dragon Room by Audrey Wood
- If you can make a special place by magic, what would it be like?

Peter's Chair by Ezra Jack Keats
- Are you a big brother or a big sister? Describe your feelings when a baby arrived in your family.

The Mitten Tree by Candace Christiansen
- Tell how you can help people in need.

When It Starts to Snow by Phillis Gershator
- Write what you like to do in snowy weather.

It's Mine by Leo Lionni
- Explain why it is important to share.

When I'm Big by Nila Aye and Tim Drury
- Tell what you want to do when you are "big."

Lester and Clyde by James H. Reece
- Describe what you can do to take care of our environment.

All the Colors of the Earth by Sheila Hamanaka
- Why do you think people look different from one another?

In My Momma's Kitchen by Jerdine Nolen
- Talk about families and family traditions.

Kitaq Goes Ice Fishing by Margaret Nicolai
- Describe a special time with a grandparent.

The Paper Crane by Molly Bang
- Describe how you would feel if something not real came to life.
- Write a story about doing nice things for other people.

Tomas and the Library Lady by Pat Mora
- Describe your favorite book and tell why you like it so much.

Management Strategies for Writing

Here are a few suggestions to help manage writing in your classroom.

Color-coded Folders

Give each student a different colored folder for each step of the writing process. It is a quick way for you to see which stage your students are working on at any given time.

Color Dot Stickers

Use a different color dot sticker for each stage of the process. The students can put these on their papers themselves. It is an easy way to track where the students are in the process.

Clip Wheel

Make a large circle out of poster board and label it with the different stages of the writing process in separate sections. Write the students' names on clothespins. The students can move their clothespins as they move through the writing process.

Portfolios

Set up portfolios to store completed writing for each student. These are great to show at open houses and conferences.

Writing Folders

Give each student a folder to store writing resource sheets—My Word List, Five Senses Word Sheets, and so on. The students can keep them in their desks for easy use.

Writing Center Material List

Writers use many tools during the writing process. It is helpful to your students to set up a writing center in the classroom where they can find the supplies they may need. This can be a table or extra desk in the corner of the room. Some examples of supplies that can be put in the writing center are

- pencils
- colored pencils
- erasers
- crayons
- markers
- scissors
- stapler
- holepunch
- tape
- glue
- glue sticks
- alphabet stamps
- picture stamps
- ink pads
- letter stencils
- stickers
- word books (lists of various nouns, verbs, adjectives)
- high-frequency word bookmarks
- dictionary
- thesaurus
- different kinds of paper (lined, unlined, construction)
- yarn/string
- a computer

Answer key

Page 87

1. My friend ^Bben likes to play with me.
2. I went to the zoo with ^Jjill.
3. We saw ^Nnick at the game.
4. On Monday, ^Mmario will go to the store.
5. We will learn about ^Cchristoper ^Ccolumbus.

Page 88

1. My family ate dinner at ^Jjim's ^Ccrab ^Sshack.
2. We went to ^Fflorida for our vacation.
3. I got a new bat and ball from ^Ssports ^Wworld.
4. The students at ^Wwest ^Eelementary ^Sschool read a lot of books.
5. My mom went to ^Oold ^Ttown ^Bbank to get some money.

Page 89

1. On ^Mmonday, we will go to the park.
2. Kim's birthday is in ^Mmarch.
3. We do not have school on ^Ssaturday or ^Ssunday.
4. The summer months are ^Jjune, ^Jjuly, and ^Aaugust.
5. José will come over on ^Ffriday to play.

Page 90

1. I went to the store. I got apples for pie.
2. Jade is good at soccer. ^Sshe scored two goals.
3. The dog has a bone. ^Sshe will bury it in the yard.
4. My favorite color is blue. I like the color green, too.

Answer key

Page 91

1. The boy likes to fish.
2. Will you take out the trash?
3. Did he get a new bike?
4. A duck is in the water.
5. Can I have some water?
6. Sam and Keisha are friends.
7. The man is on the bench.
8. When will we go to the park?
9. We will go to the zoo.
10. What is your name?

will, did, can, when, what

Page 92

1. Watch out!
2. I am going to school.
3. There are fish in the pond.
4. What a great day!
5. Tim wants to ride on the train.
6. This is fun!
7. My mom works at the library.
8. The dog wants to go for a walk.
9. Ouch, that hurts!
10. We won our game!

Page 93

1. climbed
2. hopped
3. skip
4. talked
5. finish
1. walked
2. jumped
3. leaped
4. parked
5. called

Page 94

1. talking
2. run
3. throwing
4. playing
5. wear
1. crashing
2. roaring
3. showing
4. soaring
5. seeing

144 0-7682-3101-9 *Writing: Total Solutions for Teachers*